Tibet

Tibet

AN INNER JOURNEY

Matthieu Ricard

Thames & Hudson

Contents

The Tibetans regard rainbows as auspicious. We saw this one on a summer's evening on the high plateaux inhabited by nomads in the Yerey Gang region of eastern Tibet, at 4,000 metres.

The young nomads of eastern Tibet often wear amber, coral and turquoises in their hair. Dzachuka region.

Introduction

Tibet is the Roof of the World, a place where you feel that you are in the sky just as much as you are on the earth. The intense blueness of space contrasts sharply with the deep green of eastern Tibet's rolling grasslands and the mineral colours of the west with its expanses of barren rock. Faces here are astonishingly beautiful, solid like the rocks, but as limpid as the sky. Aged monks turn huge prayer wheels with unflagging energy.

For over a thousand years, Buddhist culture has been the bedrock of Tibetan society, and anyone who has travelled across these high plateaux will understand how this contemplative civilization flourished in a landscape of such vastness.

What strikes the visitor to the Land of Snows, or anyone meeting Tibetan refugees beyond the country's borders, is the unique combination of cheerfulness, courage and deeply rooted confidence that characterizes the Tibetan people.

The old Tibet was far from perfect, based as it was on a feudal system with all its inherent social inequalities. Modern Tibet, however, is seriously in danger of losing the very essence of its culture and of drifting towards the worst and most trivial aspects of modern life.

Nevertheless, when a nation becomes a victim of crimes against humanity (more than a million Tibetans have died in the wake of the Chinese invasion) and of cultural genocide, every manifestation of its human, artistic and spiritual life assumes symbolic value and testifies to the fierce drive for survival.

For some twenty years, Tibet has been experiencing the beginning of a renaissance no less welcome for the fact that it is taking place under the yoke of a totalitarian regime. Monasteries have been rebuilt and a small number of monks and nuns have been authorized to resume their studies and spiritual practice.

This book seeks to bear witness to all that survives of that ancient world – a world capable of making a valuable contribution to contemporary life. It also aims to provide a glimpse of a unique culture that is desperately trying to preserve its authenticity, despite the major upheavals that have shaken the land of its birth.

Photography, and portrait photography most especially, is of course a form of intrusion. Spiritual masters, in particular, inspire immense respect, and it is impossible to regard them as ordinary photographic subjects. Ideally, one would like to be invisible and silent, and forfeiting the opportunity of simply living the present moment in all its fullness can be a high price to pay for taking a photograph. And yet the wish to share the richness of the lived moment may also override the desire to perpetuate that serenity for a while, and we have to resign ourselves to clicking the shutter, albeit as discreetly as possible. May the images that follow serve as a homage to inner beauty.

Young monks from Shechen monastery in eastern Tibet. They receive a basic education at the monastery and only take their monastic vows, if they wish to do so, at the age of twenty.

A Traditional Society

Khyentse Rinpoche (1910–91), one of the principal masters of the Ancient (Nyingma) Tradition of Tibetan Buddhism. He is seen here at dawn in the monastery of Shechen, on the final day of a ceremony that is carried out day and night for one week. Nepal, 1987.

A Traditional Society

The ancient, traditional Tibet is now intermingling with a Tibet in transition, victim of a military invasion that has cost the lives of more than a million Tibetans and continues to pose a major threat to its culture and values. The progressive watering down of the Tibetan language and its literature and the massive deforestation and extinction of wildlife due to China's intervention are matters of grave concern. The Tibetans are themselves caught up in this process, in some cases regretting it, in others playing the game of assimilating the Chinese way of life and adapting to the modern world in all its aspects, both positive and negative.

In this book I have sought to illustrate the surviving elements of traditional Tibet: its spirituality, the purity and grandeur of its landscape, its festivals and its nomadic and peasant populations. Buddhism has been the foundation of Tibetan society for over a thousand years. Prior to the Chinese invasion, monks, nuns, hermits and scholars represented a quarter of the entire population – a unique situation in the history of humanity. At that time the Land of Snows harboured more than six thousand monasteries, not to mention countless temples and hermitages. Spiritual practice was at the very centre of everyday life, and the lay population itself – nomads, farmers and merchants – regarded their ordinary activities, however necessary, as secondary in importance to the study and practice of the teachings of the Buddha. As a result, Tibetan Buddhism has given rise to a great number of remarkable men and women who, as living examples of the potential for human perfection, have been a constant source of inspiration to the community at whose heart they once lived.

Things were far from perfect in the old Tibet: peasants were exploited by the nobility; crimes elicited inhumane punishments; medieval-style intrigues were rife, along with other vices typical of feudal society. And yet the unique civilization that flourished in Tibet continues to this day to inspire the rest of the world with its wisdom, its sheer joie de vivre, its ideal of inner transformation and its culture of non-violence, values that have remained predominant despite some unfortunate departures from the ideal path.

THE PRESENCE OF THE MONASTERIES

The monastery is a place brimming with life and open to all and sundry. One of its primary purposes is the education of young men or women who demonstrate a propensity for philosophical study or the pursuit of a contemplative life. It may also encompass an art school where, alongside painting and sculpture, students are taught to make costumes for the ritual dances. Sacred art illustrates symbols and ideas that serve as an aid to understanding the meaning of Buddhist teachings. It can provide a direct experience of inner peace and facilitate progress along the spiritual path.

The rituals are magnificent events that frequently last for an entire day and, in some cases, can continue for nine days and nine nights without interruption. The liturgy is sung in a soft, solemn voice and broken by periods of silence, during which the participants inwardly recite mantras (sacred formulas that subtly affect the participants' mental state), and by musical offerings in which the sounds of long horns, bells and tambourines intermingle.

These ceremonies sometimes end with dances that are in themselves living illustrations of the teachings. In the West, dance is often the expression of strong emotions that are very far removed from monastic preoccupations. These sacred dances, by contrast, serve to calm negative emotions and increase a sense of profound wellbeing. They are a form of meditation through movement and a means of spiritual sharing within the Buddhist community.

THE POWER OF TRANSMISSION

The transmission of spiritual teachings from a master to a disciple guarantees the vitality and authenticity of the Buddhist tradition. Its purpose is to allow students access to the philosophical texts and to introduce them to various meditation techniques. The accompanying explanations may sometimes last for weeks. As part of the process of transmission, a qualified master also gives personal instruction that is adapted to the individual's spiritual needs and to the level attained on the spiritual path. The importance of this transmission brings with it a profound respect for the teacher and for the bond thus forged with him. By the force of his example, a true spiritual master demonstrates to his disciple what he himself could become.

SPIRITUAL PRACTICE

To meditate is to familiarize ourselves with a new way of looking at things. It is also a means of cultivating essential human qualities in the long term. The aim of meditation is to increase healthy emotions such as empathy, compassion and love of others and progressively to eliminate the mental poisons of hatred, desire, jealousy and arrogance. Meditation also helps to develop greater clarity of thinking, so enabling us to reduce the gap between reality and the false ideas which we project on to it.

Meditation on compassion and altruistic love, for example, consists in focusing attention on the suffering of sentient beings, recognizing that all such beings aspire to happiness and have no wish to suffer, then in placing ourselves in a mental state where nothing else exists but this compassion and love for our fellow beings, both those close to us and those who are strangers or enemies, both humans and animals. This compassion is totally inclusive, and from it is born a feeling of universal love, and responsibility and respect for each and every being. Like the two wings of a bird, compassion and wisdom are indivisible: knowledge without compassion is sterile, and compassion without knowledge is blind.

SACRED GEOGRAPHY AND THE ENVIRONMENT IN DANGER

Tibet is a landscape of such immensity and spectacular beauty that we can readily understand how it gave birth to a civilization whose whole focus is contemplative. The Tibetans have a long-held and profound respect for nature. According to their sacred geography, mountains, forests, lakes and rivers are home to local deities and places blessed by the spiritual masters of the past, and as such they inspire respect. A sacred lake should not be polluted, a sacred forest should not be cut down, and a sacred mountain should not be exploited for its mineral resources. Nor is it permissible to hunt or fish in these localities, since to do so would undermine the beneficial influence that these places exert on the peace and prosperity of the region's inhabitants.

The Chinese invasion of Tibet was followed by intense exploitation of the country's natural resources, leading to the deforestation of 40 per cent of Tibet's woodlands and the almost total extermination of its wildlife. At the present time, the Tibetans themselves are also guilty of failing in their respect for the natural environment. Plastic bags and beer bottles litter the grasslands near inhabited areas, and adults and children spend part of the summer months digging up cordyceps mushrooms, or *yartsa gonbu* (meaning 'plant in summer, worms in winter'), for which the Chinese pay very high prices and which are sold for their dubious medicinal and aphrodisiac properties. The skins of leopards, tigers, snow leopards, otters and other rare and protected species are openly sold on the street, in defiance of international prohibitions and Chinese laws which the corrupt authorities seem reluctant to enforce. The Dalai Lama recently denounced the recent Tibetan custom of wearing coats trimmed with fur taken from panthers, tigers and snow leopards; a fashion, he explained, that was in total contradiction to the Buddhist ideal of compassion. Following his injunction, in January 2005, a great many Tibetans publicly burned their furs.

HOPES AND FEARS

Tibetan traditions are threatened not only from outside, but from inside too. Visitors to present-day Tibet are likely to witness a disconcerting mix of the bizarrely modern and the archaically superstitious. In the vicinity of a large village, it is not uncommon to see nomads on horseback rummaging in the depths of their sheepskin coats and pulling out mobile phones with loud ringtones. Nomad tents are lit at night by the faint gleam of lamps powered by solar panels. In village homes, television sets churn out Chinese melodramas as vulgar as they are violent.

Many young Tibetans can no longer speak their own language fluently. In town, and especially in official circles, Chinese is more likely to be heard than Tibetan. Peasants and nomads, by contrast, can barely mumble a few words of Chinese, and for this reason are excluded from secondary schools and from expensive university courses at the universities of Lhasa, Xining and Chengdu. The official education system is biased towards the promotion of the

13

Chinese language. While Tibetan still plays an important role at primary level, at secondary level Chinese becomes the principal vehicle for instructional purposes and the only language permitted in examinations.

Is the real Tibet actually located in the exiled communities of India, Nepal and elsewhere? On the occasion of the United Nations' 50th anniversary, the expatriate Tibetan community was held up as a model example of its kind. Since its inception, the government in exile has devoted, and continues to devote, 30 per cent of its budget to education. Indeed, the preservation of Tibetan culture has remained an absolute priority. Inspired by the admirable example of the Dalai Lama, all these exiles, monks, nuns, scholars, hermits, lay men and women, have done an extraordinary job of safeguarding their language and their art, alongside the values and traditions, both academic and contemplative, that make up Buddhist culture. But the diaspora only represents a sixtieth of the Tibetan population and is submerged in the midst of foreign cultures. For geographic, historical and ethnic reasons, the high plateaux of the Roof of the World where six million Tibetans live, in other words more than 95 per cent of the population, will always be Tibet, whatever fate befalls it. We shall need to count therefore on the strength of mind and the determination of the Tibetans themselves, the renaissance of philosophy schools and centres of meditation, and the enlightened support of free peoples. The clock is ticking for Tibet: let us hope that it may soon mark the dawn of Tibetan recovery.

Lighted candles at the Bodnath stupa near Kathmandu, placed there by Nepal's Tibetan Buddhist community in memory of the victims of the tsunami on 26 December 2004. Although Nepal is one of the poorest countries in the world, it donated more than a million dollars to the disaster fund.

In the courtyard of a temple dating from the 7th century, at Paro Kyichu in Bhutan, the young Tibetan lama Shechen Rabjam Rinpoche is performing a fire offering ceremony, during which consecrated substances are offered to the deities of a mandala visualized in the 'fire of wisdom', 1985.

Khyentse Rinpoche, one of Tibet's greatest spiritual masters, and also one of the Dalai Lama's masters, surrounded by *tulku* (reincarnated lamas) in front of the great stupa at Bodnath, Nepal. The purpose of this gathering, in 1977, was to receive a vast cycle of teachings and initiations from Khyentse Rinpoche.

A teacher explains aspects of the Buddhist texts to monks at the philosophy school at Sakar monastery, in Kham, eastern Tibet.

These huge prayer wheels each contain around a hundred million mantras and prayers printed in tiny letters on great sheets of paper rolled around the central axle of the wheel. The monks spin the wheels as they walk past, while praying for the good of all beings. Lagong monastery, Minyak province, Kham, eastern Tibet.

Ornamental banners and monks at prayer in the main temple of Sera monastery, near Lhasa, central Tibet, 2004.

Opposite:

On his return to eastern Tibet, Dzongsar Khyentse Rinpoche is greeted by a procession at the entrance to his monastery.

Overleaf:

Left: Monks from the philosophy school at Dzongsar monastery, in eastern Tibet, engaging in lively debates at the end of the afternoon.

Right: These debates focus on philosophical questions which the monks have been studying in the course of the day. This monastery was completely destroyed during the Cultural Revolution and partially rebuilt by the local people.

Opposite:

Peasant family from the village of Sakar, eastern Tibet.

Right:

Elderly people in Tibet devote most of their
time to prayer and meditation. Eastern Tibet.

The head of Dzagyal monastery greeting a visitor, Dzachuka province, eastern Tibet.

Left:
Young novice monks are surprised and delighted to see themselves on a video screen. Bumnying monastery, Dzachuka, eastern Tibet.

Overleaf, from left to right:
Young novice at Shechen monastery, eastern Tibet.
Young nomad girl, photographed near Mount Kailash. This little girl lived with her mother and father in a remote corner of western Tibet, where the family ran a small inn. The sign outside read simply: 'Tea and yoghurt'.
This young monk lives with his uncle, a wandering monk, in eastern Tibet.
A young lama identified as the reincarnation of a great master, on the day of his enthronement ceremony at the Tibetan monastery of Shechen in Nepal.

Young boy learning to read in one of our schools in Sakar, eastern Tibet.

Opposite:
A young boy and girl at the school in Gemang, in eastern Tibet, one of those supported by our humanitarian programmes (Shechen and Karuna).
Before the school was built, the local nomad children received no education.

Overleaf:
Left: Little nomad girl from the Tsatsa region, eastern Tibet.
Right: A doctor takes the pulse of a nomad girl from Tsatsa in a clinic supported by our humanitarian programme, eastern Tibet.

An elderly nun and a Tibetan peasant family from the village of Sakar, gathered together at home in the presence of a visiting monk, eastern Tibet.

An old man spins his prayer wheel in the great
kitchens at Shechen monastery, eastern Tibet.

Young nomad girl preparing cheese inside her hut. Dzongsar region, eastern Tibet.

A nomad woman in front of her hearth. An opening has been made in the centre of the tent of woven yak hair to allow the smoke to escape.
The fire of dried yak dung burns night and day. Kham, eastern Tibet.

Left:
A woman from Kham with her child, Dzongsar valley,
eastern Tibet.

Opposite:
A Tibetan nomad woman milking a *dri* (female yak) in Dzogchen
valley, at 4,200 metres. Province of Kham, eastern Tibet (now
part of the Chinese province of Sichuan).

Herd of yaks led by riders, near Shechen monastery, eastern Tibet.

During the autumn migration, the nomads of eastern Tibet leave the high pastures (4,300–4,800 m) for grazing grounds situated between 4,000 and 3,800 m, where they spend the months of September and October before returning to their winter quarters.

Nomad from the sacred valley of Dakpa Lhari, to the south of Lithang, eastern Tibet.

Right:
Dzagyal monastery in the province of Dzachuka, seen in July, when the high meadows (here 4,200 metres) are studded
with golden yellow flowers. The monastery belongs to the Nyingmapa school of Tibetan Buddhism.

Overleaf:
A Buddhist convent in Gemang in Dzachuka province, eastern Tibet.

In the Tawu region of eastern Tibet, grassy hillsides give way to curious formations of rock and black sand, spattered with white mineral salts.

A Major Pilgrimage Every Twelve Years

48 Three monks travelling from Amdo, in north-east Tibet, to the holy city of Lhasa, a journey of over a thousand kilometres. Every three steps, they lie down on the path, so that the length of the route becomes a multiple of the length of their own bodies. It will take them a year to reach Lhasa. Their few belongings and some food are carried in a small cart which one of the three goes back to fetch every hundred metres. They generally sleep under the stars, even when there is snow on the ground, and they live off *tsampa*, roasted barley flour, mixed with butter tea. In the course of a month's travelling in Kham, we met them three times. Twice we gave them a small gift of money, but when we offered a third time they refused, saying that they had no need of anything.

A Major Pilgrimage Every Twelve Years

FROM THE 'CRYSTAL CAVE' TO THE 'LAKE OF TURQUOISE WHERE THE SNOW LIONESS ROARS'

In Tibet there are many sacred places that serve as pilgrimage sites. According to the Tibetan calendar, one year in every twelve is particularly propitious for making a pilgrimage. This calendar is based on a twelve-year cycle. Each cycle is symbolized by an animal: bird, dragon, dog, monkey, and so on, and each of these is linked with one of the five elements – water, earth, wood, iron and fire – to give a major cycle of sixty years, the Tibetan and Chinese equivalent of our century.

Accordingly, in the year of the Wooden Monkey (the last was in 2004), hundreds of pilgrims come pouring into the lush valley of Dzongsar, in eastern Tibet. A three-day walk will take them to its holy places (all of them situated at high altitude): Detchen Pema Shelphuk, 'the Crystal Cave of the Lotus of Great Bliss', Karmo Taksang, 'the White Lair of the Tiger', and Seng-ngu Yutso, 'the Lake of Turquoise where the Snow Lioness Roars'. Pilgrimages are traditionally made on foot, though the less hardy may sometimes cover part of the route on horseback.

A day's walk from Dzongsar, the pilgrims spend their first night at Dophu, a delightful valley where a crystal-clear river wends its way through flowering meadows. Setting off again at dawn, with a light blanket and a handful of provisions, they spend the first two hours of the morning climbing a wooded rise.

The ascent above the treeline is steeper and involves zigzagging back and forth for an hour across a slope littered with rocks and the odd juniper bush that has managed to survive despite the altitude of over 4,000 metres. Then come the first high-mountain flowers, such as the meconopsis, whose beautiful yellow bloom, resembling a tulip with narrow closed petals, hangs from its tall stem like a hanging reliquary – hence its Tibetan name, *gaochung*, meaning 'little reliquary'. A couple of great ravens – twice the size of our own crows, a species that has almost disappeared in Europe – settle next to us for a moment, then fly off again with a series of grave and sonorous croaks that echo from the mountain slopes. A lammergeyer, with a brilliant orange head, hovers high above us.

When we finally arrive at the pass, the view that meets our eyes is of range after range of mountains spreading in all directions, the furthest peaks almost indistinguishable from the blue of the sky. Instead of descending, however, we now have to cut across the slope by traversing piles of fallen rock of all sizes, jumbled together higgledy-piggledy and alternating with glittering slopes of slate which give way underfoot and threaten to pitch us back down the mountain. Poking through here and there are curious succulent plants with purple flowers and furry leaves and clumps of brilliant green moss starred with tiny white flowers, and also a few rare medicinal plants, whose properties are described to us by Lodrö, a renowned Tibetan doctor who is acting as our guide. We are almost at 5,000 metres at this point, walking more slowly and breathing harder. After picking our way across the slope for an hour, we arrive at last at the entrance to the cirque that cradles 'the Lake of Turquoise where the Snow Lioness Roars'.

The lake is said to be the home of a powerful guardian spirit, a *naga*, half-man, half-serpent, who has appeared at its surface on several occasions when great masters have visited. On a bright day, the waters are a dazzling turquoise blue which veers to pale green, or black, when the sky clouds over. The cirque is a configuration of sharp ridges whose rock-strewn sides fall steeply to the lake. To the south-east, a barrier of rocks, surrounded by little meadows, holds back the waters, which overflow towards the valley through a series of gullies. A path encircles the lake, enabling pilgrims to walk around it respectfully while reciting prayers and mantras.

At the bottom of the cirque, on a shelf overhanging the lake by some twenty metres, are three tiny hermitages built of large flat stones, so small inside that they can only accommodate one person in a sitting position. A number of spiritual teachers have spent their time on retreat in these holy places, in particular the great master Jamyang Khyentse Wangpo, who was profoundly influential in the 19th century and contributed to the preservation of Tibetan Buddhism at a time when the transmission of many of its teachings was in danger of being disrupted. 'In November 1866', Lodrö tells us,

'Khyentse Wangpo came to the edge of this lake, accompanied by another celebrated master, Chogyur Lingpa, along with the King of Derge and some hundred followers. The lake was frozen except at its centre, where the ice opened like a window, around which the company gathered in a circle. It was there that the *naga*, the guardian spirit of the lake, presented to Chogyur Lingpa a gold reliquary containing precious teachings that had come from Padmasambhava, the master who led the rise of Buddhism in Tibet in the 8th and 9th centuries.'

A handful of pilgrims have assembled on the strip of ground at the entrance to the lake to make an offering of incense. Thick scented swirls of smoke rise up from branches of juniper dipped in lake water. The pilgrims visualize the smoke as offerings of flowers and jewels, food and perfumes presented to the Buddhas and to the guardian spirits of the site, and pray that all living beings may be delivered from suffering and come to know peace and prosperity.

There is no time to linger: we need to reach our next stopping place before nightfall. We take the descent into the valley almost at a run and, an hour later, we reach Karmo Taksang, 'the White Lair of the Tiger'. The hermitage here is a temple surrounded by a dozen cells clinging to a little cliff in the middle of the forest. To the uninformed this hermitage looks like any other, but it has a particularly rich history. It was here, notably, that the master Mipham Rinpoche, one of the greatest yogis and scholars Tibet has known, spent thirteen

years in total solitude. During that time, he produced a series of contemplative writings, from which the following lines are taken:

When the waves of thoughts
Affect the peace of our minds no more
Than clouds alter the sky,
This is called 'liberation of thoughts in their true nature'.

A dozen practitioners are currently undertaking a five-year retreat at Karmo Taksang.

We are restored by our night's sleep here, lying side by side in two wooden huts, one of which was erected on the site of Mipham Rinpoche's original hermitage. Then, early the next morning, we set off again, climbing through flower-filled meadows to the pass that will take us to Pema Shelphuk. We have a long rest at the top, exhausted by the climb, but enchanted by the sweeping views. From here, we follow a long ridge. The Crystal Cave lies below us, in the middle of a lush green cirque which the sacred texts compare to a lotus of light, fully open and perfectly formed. The cave itself is in one of the two large rocks in the shape of a sugar loaf which tower over the dark green of the forests like two granite jewels illuminated by the midday sun.

An endless line of pilgrims is circling round the holy site – it takes about half an hour to complete the circuit – while others are resting and recovering in the meadow that overlooks the cave. It is not uncommon for pilgrims to remain here for several days in order to complete the circuit a hundred times, a devotional practice said to be of great merit.

The main cave opens in the southern face of the rocks. The way in is through a small temple built at its entrance. The cave is enormous, its roof covered with a multitude of rock crystals. On an altar stands a statue of the 'Master of Great Bliss', one of the many aspects of Guru Padmasambhava. A few rugs have been thrown on the ground so that practitioners – monks, nuns, hermits and passing pilgrims – can meditate and make ritual offerings in greater comfort. It was here, in this cave, during the winter of 1856, that the two visionary masters Chogyur Lingpa and Khyentse Wangpo revealed the spiritual treasure known as 'the Three Sections of the Great Perfection', which contains profound teachings on the means of liberating oneself from negative emotions by recognizing the ultimate nature of mind. This place is regarded as one of the holiest in all of Tibet.

After spending a few hours meditating and accompanying the pilgrims in their circumambulations, it is time to return to the valley if we wish to reach the monastery of Dzongsar before nightfall. During the descent, we stop for a few moments beside some trees surrounded with a number of flat stones engraved with mantras, where the great translator Verotsana meditated. Old men and women from the neighbouring village, lacking the strength to climb up as far as the Crystal Cave, are walking in respectful procession round this holy place, hour after hour, holding a prayer wheel in one hand and a *mala*, the Buddhist rosary, in the other. Their faces, etched by the sun's rays and the rigours of the Tibetan winter, have an openness and a smiling radiance that lights them up and goes straight to our hearts. After walking along the river for a few kilometres, we are soon back at the monastery, exhausted but filled with a new inner peace.

In the year of the Wooden Bird (2005), it is the turn of Tongkor, a holy site near Gantze, in western Tibet, to receive the homages of several thousand pilgrims. The site is a configuration of three holy mountains which the pilgrims circumambulate in the course of a three-hour walk. Many of them take a vow to repeat this circumambulation, or *khora*, thirteen times. In some cases, their dedication is such that they will undertake the *khora*, regardless of the weather, by prostrating themselves on the path, so that the length of the circuit becomes a multiple of the length of their own bodies. The path is littered with prayer flags hung from the trees and the rocks, with caves where masters have meditated in the past and with stones engraved with mantras piled into cairns. In the evening, the pilgrims camp together at the intersection of the the paths. They leave the next day, at dawn, full of eagerness, radiating an inner peace, for a long day of walking and prayers.

Founded in the 7th century by Padmasambhava, under the patronage of King Trison Detsen, Samye was the first large Buddhist monastery to be built in Tibet. On his return to Tibet in 1985, Dilgo Khyentse Rinpoche (1910–91) asked the Chinese government for permission to restore the monastery. Surprisingly, his request was granted. Restorations of the main temple were completed in 1990 and Khyentse Rinpoche was invited to perform the consecration ceremony.

Tsetsam Ani, a Tibetan nun who has spent forty-five years on retreat in her hermitage at Debuche, Nepal. This was the first time she had ever allowed herself to be photographed and she told us that she would not allow anyone to do so thereafter.

Left:
Buddhists visit all the great Tibetan pilgrimage sites regularly. Each site becomes the focus of a special pilgrimage every twelve years, which corresponds to a particular year in the Tibetan lunar calendar. During the year of the Wooden Bird (2005), it was the turn of Tongkor, near Gantze, in eastern Tibet, to receive the homage of thousands of pilgrims. On these occasions, it is customary to drape prayer flags from trees and rocks all along the route.

Overleaf:
The three monks en route from Amdo, in north-east Tibet, to the holy city of Lhasa, doing prostrations all the way.

Above and opposite:
A mother and her child camp for several days at the start of the route that leads around the holy site.

Situated in the middle of the great loop of the Brahmaputra river, the snow-covered summit of Namchak Barwa rises to 7,756 m. Here, the majestic river, known in Tibet as the Tsangpo, carves its way through the mountains to emerge again 150 km away and 2,700 m lower. Until the end of the 20th century, the Namchak Barwa was one of the world's last unexplored places. It was only in 1998 that American explorers discovered the legendary 'Hidden Falls', whose existence had long been suspected.

Prayer flags are scattered over an entire hillside near the monastery of Lagong, in Minyak province, Kham, eastern Tibet. Prayers and sacred images are printed on the flags, and the wind that touches them is said to carry the blessings of these invocations to all the beings that it encounters.

A forest of prayer flags in the Golok region. Other natural elements are used for a similar purpose: prayers are engraved on rocks, streams are used for turning prayer wheels, and the warm air generated by butter-lamp flames serves to turn little paper windmills.

During the Tongkor pilgrimage, a monk scatters blessings printed on little squares of multicoloured paper (*lungta*).
He is almost lost in a sea of prayer flags that have been draped from trees growing at the top of a pass.

Above and opposite:
Pilgrims respectfully circumambulate Tongkor's three holy mountains by prostrating themselves along the path. In general, those who choose to walk normally take a vow to complete the circuit (*khora* in Tibetan) thirteen times.

The monastery-palace of Yumbu Lakhang, the seat of the first kings of Tibet.
It was destroyed during the Chinese invasion and rebuilt in the 1990s.

Samye monastery, one of the main pilgrimage sites in central Tibet. It was the first of Tibet's large monasteries,
built under the auspices of Guru Padmasambhava, the 'Lotus-Born Master'.

A pilgrim attaches prayer flags to the summit of the Drolma La (5,860 m), eastern Tibet. The pass is the culmination of the Mount Kailash circuit.

This little girl has come with her family for the Tongkor pilgrimage.

The sacred lake of Seng-ngu Yutso, the 'Lake of Turquoise where the Snow Lioness Roars',
which lies 5,000 m above the monastery of Dzongsar. Every twelve years, the lake becomes the
focus of a special pilgrimage.

Opposite:
A woman has climbed up to one of the many caves that litter the Tongkor route. This photograph was taken in the late afternoon.

Overleaf:
Panoramic view of the rocks and sacred caves of the 'Crystal Cave' (Pema Shelphuk) above the monastery of Dzongsar, in eastern Tibet.
The cave attracted a great many pilgrims in 2004, the year of the Wooden Monkey.

Monks play sacred music while the crowd waits to greet a reincarnated lama on his return to the monastery of Dzongsar.

The Return of a Spiritual Master

Khyentse Rinpoche crossing the White Horses pass (Gose La), at 5,000 m. It is said that even if they are black when you begin the climb, your horses will be white once you reach the top. Khyentse Rinpoche travelled in a chair carried by local nomads, who regarded it as an honour to carry their spiritual master and were impatient to change places every quarter of an hour. They walked so fast that the rest of our group, who had come from India, struggled to keep up with them, even though we had nothing to carry. Derge province, eastern Tibet, 1987.

The Return of a Spiritual Master

'The lama is coming back!' The long-awaited news has spread like wildfire and thousands of peasants and nomads have come to greet the spiritual master. Some of them, from neighbouring valleys, have been riding for days; others have come down from the high pastures, lying at over 4,500 metres, where they take their yak herds in the summer months. They have left other members of their family in charge of the animals, and tomorrow these shepherds will hurry back up to the pastures so that their relatives can come down in their turn to receive the lama's blessing.

Hundreds of tents have been erected on a huge plain, next to the river. The tents have been woven out of thick white cotton decorated with arabesques made from bands of black fabric sewn by hand. The largest are the size of a circus big top and can accommodate several hundred people. One of them in particular is attracting the crowds: this is the tent where the lama will be spending his time in the days to come.

A few riders who had gone off to meet the master come galloping onto the plain: 'They're coming! They've already passed the Mechö bridge!' Everyone gets busy. The monks assemble their telescopic horns (a four-metre musical instrument) and adjust the mouthpiece of their *gyaling*, a sort of oboe made of red sandalwood inlaid with gold and silver. The welcoming procession positions itself amid a great deal of noise and confusion.

A hundred or so riders arrive, sitting proudly on their mounts and dressed in festive costume – baggy trousers in white wild silk, brown woollen coats and scarlet turbans. They are brandishing standards and banners that float in the wind as they gallop towards the tents, dispersing the clouds of scented white smoke rising from the many fires of juniper branches which the crowd have lit. To the amusement of the onlookers, some of the horses rear and others try to bolt – but it takes more than that to unseat a rider from Kham.

Then there are cries of 'Here he is!' The lama arrives mounted on a brown horse caparisoned with brocades and silk scarves, its mane and tail wound with multicoloured ribbons. He changed his mode of transport a few miles back, abandoning the jeep he had been travelling in for three days since leaving the plains of China.

The lama's name is Dzongsar Jamyang Khyentse Rinpoche and he has come from Bhutan, where he lives for part of the year. He is the head of Dzongsar monastery, but he has not been able to go back there for a long time. The deep devotion felt by the people of this region for Jamyang Khyentse stems from the fact that this forty-four-year-old lama is the reincarnation of one of the most venerated masters in the whole of Tibet, Jamyang Khyentse Chökyi Lodrö, who died in India in 1959 after fleeing the Chinese invasion.

A huge crowd pushes forward in an attempt to get close to the procession. The locals, massed on either side of the path, bow respectfully to the lama as he passes and throw flowers as a gesture of welcome. During the three days of festivities in his honour, they will literally feast on his presence. The lama, preceded by the monk-musicians, is at the heart of the procession escorted by the riders who carve a path through the human tide. He arrives at last at the tent where he will rest for a short while before giving his blessing to all those who have come to meet him.

Several thousand nomads are now seated in the meadow in front of the lama's tent. The latter takes his place on a simple seat and, with the help of a battery-operated loudspeaker provided by the monastery, he offers his greetings to the assembled crowd. He gives them a few spiritual instructions and also some simple advice, urging each of them to avoid quarrelling at all costs (a common failing among these nomads). He asks if any of them are ready to give up alcohol, and half the crowd raise their hands as a sign that they are; to give up smoking (almost everyone raises their hand); to give up hunting and to protect the environment and refrain from littering the countryside with plastic bags (again the majority agree). The exchange is good-natured, even humorous. There is much laughter about who is promising to do what, or not promising, as the case may be.

The blessing follows, and the tone is now more serious. The lama recites a sacred text and carries out a preliminary ritual. He stands up and, preceded by a monk who opens a pathway in front of him by swinging incense sticks and a white silk ceremonial scarf from right to left, passes slowly down the lines, placing a blessed object on the head of each person.

During this two-hour ceremony, two monks play their oboes continuously. The musicians use a special technique called 'circular breathing' which allows them to blow into the instrument without stopping. This involves gradually expelling a pocket of air formed by expanding the cheeks, while inhaling through the nostrils to inflate the lungs. To anyone unfamiliar with this technique it always seems quite astonishing to hear these monks holding a continuous note for more than ten minutes at a stretch.

Pathways open up spontaneously in the crowd and two or three lines of kneeling participants receive the blessings together. Men, women, children and old folk sometimes fall on top of one another. Their eyes are shining with a mixture of joy and reverence. Some of them recite prayers out loud, praying for the happiness of all living beings and a long life for the lama.

The afternoon is drawing to a close. The lama makes his way now to the monastery, where he will spend the night. Once more, people form a long procession, preparing to accompany him on the two-kilometre journey between the improvised camp and the hill on which the monastery (restored over the last fifteen years) stands. Shortly before arriving, the lama dismounts and, out of respect for the sacredness of the place and for all the great masters who have lived there in the past, he covers the last hundred metres on foot. Then, still preceded by the musicians and monks carrying banners, he enters the narrow alleyways that lead to his residence. The festivities will continue for another two days with equestrian games, folk dancing and, once again, blessings distributed to the crowd.

Almost twenty years ago, in 1988, Dzongsar Jamyang Khyentse Rinpoche arrived in Tibet for the first time, in very different circumstances. He was twenty-seven and was accompanying his own spiritual master, Dilgo Khyentse Rinpoche, one of the most eminent masters of 20th-century Tibetan Buddhism. The latter was returning to Tibet after more than thirty years' exile in India, Nepal and Bhutan. He was accompanied by several lamas, including his grandson Rabjam Rinpoche, his spiritual heir and the abbot of Shechen monastery.

Everywhere he went, Dilgo Khyentse Rinpoche was greeted with extraordinary fervour. For the Tibetans, his visit held tremendous significance. Many who saw him could not believe their eyes. Many shouted: 'It must be a dream!' During the thirty years of his absence, his fellow Tibetans had persevered in the face of great suffering, their faith and their determination remaining intact and unshakeable. Now, as they received the lama's blessing, the majority of them, especially the older ones, broke down in tears. Dilgo Khyentse Rinpoche smiled at them. Here and there, he recognized a familiar face. Everyone had so much to tell him: about the ordeals inflicted by the Chinese Communists, and the names of those who had perished and of those who had survived.

In addition to visiting his own monastery at Shechen, Dilgo Khyentse Rinpoche had agreed to go wherever circumstances permitted. When there was no road, he travelled in a litter or a sedan chair. For several days in succession, the company had crossed passes of over 5,000 metres, skirted precipices and waded through rivers, but all of them had wished to share the honour of carrying Khyentse Rinpoche on their shoulders. By switching carriers every quarter of an hour, they were able to cover the long distances with great speed. In front of each monastery, the lama was received in the same dignified and elaborate manner. In each case, the local population and the monks, wearing white hats as a sign of welcome, formed a long procession, headed by the musicians dressed in their brightly coloured costumes.

When Dilgo Khyentse Rinpoche and his retinue arrived at the same monastery of Dzongsar (practically in ruins at the time), a thousand riders were waiting for them. (It is worth remembering at this point that more than six thousand monasteries were destroyed following the Chinese invasion.) As the company emerged from the pass, they were met by the extraordinary sight of all these riders, ranged in a semi-circle in a meadow, each of them dismounted out of respect for the lama and holding his horse by its bridle.

Just as the procession was approaching the monastery doors, everyone suddenly looked up at the sky, where the perfect circle of a halo of rainbow light had formed around the sun – a sign which the Tibetans regard as highly propitious. And the day before, just as Dilgo Khyentse Rinpoche arrived, a double rainbow had appeared over the roofs of Palpung monastery.

Wherever he went, Khyentse Rinpoche had offered teachings, comfort and inspiration to those who had come to see him. He had reminded them that lasting happiness can only come from inner peace and that this peace, in turn, can only arise where egoism, hatred and greed are eliminated, and where altruism, love and compassion are allowed to grow and flourish.

A young monk from Shechen monastery helps to carry this musical instrument comprising a spectacular pair of telescopic horns. When they are fully extended, the metal horns are four metres in length. Eastern Tibet.

Dilgo Khyentse Rinpoche and a group of lamas at the end of a ceremony that has lasted nine days and nine nights without interruption, in the mountainous valley of Bumthang, in Bhutan. Having created the ritual mandala using coloured powder, they are now preparing to scatter the powder in the river. By destroying the mandala in this way they are symbolizing the ephemeral nature of all things.

Dilgo Khyentse Rinpoche and his entourage crossing the Tsangpo (Brahmaputra) in a flat-bottomed boat on his first return to Tibet in 1985 after more than thirty years in exile. They are on their way to the monastery of Samye.

Where the path runs out, Khyentse Rinpoche is transported by litter. Here, his group cross the river below Shechen monastery, preceded by a monk carrying a brocade parasol as a sign of honour.

These pilgrims are waiting for a visiting lama to come by. The photograph was taken near the hermitage of Jimnak Trakar in the Yerey Gang region.

This man is part of a procession of motorcyclists who have come to greet a lama on his way to Shona monastery.

A procession of riders in festive costumes comes to greet the lama.

Motorcyclists participating in the welcome procession held for a visiting lama at Mani Palgey.

Above and opposite:
Joy and devotion are evident in the faces of the crowd as they listen to the master's teachings.

At the end of a day of festivities in the adjoining meadows, Dzongsar Khyentse Rinpoche and his monks return in procession to the monastery. Dzongsar monastery was totally destroyed during the Cultural Revolution. The local population began rebuilding it in 1980.

Left:
Dzongsar Khyentse Rinpoche approaches a small monastery near Dzongsar whose monks have invited him to bless the site.
Two villagers in festive costume hold his horse by its bridle.

Overleaf:
Children among the crowd that have gathered to listen to their spiritual master.

Sitting on an improvised throne, Rabjam Rinpoche gives spiritual instruction and blessings to the monks and faithful gathered together at Gemang monastery, in Dzachuka province.

Opposite:
Rabjam Rinpoche visits Gemang monastery, in eastern Tibet, where a carpet has been unfurled in his honour.

Overleaf:
Dzongsar Khyentse Rinpoche gives a name to a newborn child, whom he blesses after cutting a lock of the child's hair, a ritual gesture symbolizing
the offering up of the highest part of the body, the top of the head. A nomad family watch what he is doing with great interest.

Monks from Shechen monastery, their cheeks reddened by the icy wind, wearing their traditional white cotton and bamboo hats as a sign of welcome. These riders have come in procession to greet Dilgo Khyentse Rinpoche – on his return to eastern Tibet in 1985 after more than thirty years in exile – and escort him on the last five kilometres of the route to the monastery.

Opposite:
This man from Kham has come with the rest of this crowd to greet Dilgo Khyentse Rinpoche. His face expresses all the devotion and courage of a people who have succeeded in preserving their dignity and their strength of purpose in the face of overwhelming tragedy.

Overleaf:
Inhabitants of Dzongsar valley, delighted by the return of their spiritual master.

Young Tibetan girl from Shechen valley.

Right and overleaf:
Nomad riders from Dzongsar valley receiving their spiritual master in grand style.
The scenes are like something from another age.

During the festival dedicated to the legendary Gesar of Ling, masked dances performed by monks re-enact the great episodes in the king's life. This was the first time that the festival of Mani Genkok had taken place in ten years.

A Sense of Celebration

This young Tibetan girl from Dzongsar valley has come to take part in the great festival of Mani Genkok and is wearing her family's finest treasures.

A Sense of Celebration

We are on our way to Mani Genkok, a large village that lies on the edge of a huge expanse of grasslands surrounded by high mountains. This morning, our jeep's radiator began to overheat. Every fifteen kilometres or so, our driver, who is a monk, kept stopping to unscrew the cap gingerly with a rag, then stand back quickly as a geyser of boiling water shot into the air. We finally realized that the radiator had a hole in it. Our ever-resourceful driver slipped into a meadow full of buttercups and came back, a few moments later, with a big grin on his face and a large handful of horse dung, which he then used to stuff the hole. We can imagine what a garage mechanic would have made of this! Unbelievably, it seems to work – for a short time, anyway. A dozen kilometres further on, the whole lot begins to bubble and boil, and an interesting mixture spurts out of the radiator! And there is no alternative but to blow into the radiator as hard as we can to clean it out.

Somehow or other, we reach Mani Genkok by the afternoon. We are going to a big three-day festival. The last time a festival like this was put on was ten years ago. This year's festival is dedicated to the legendary King Gesar of Ling and has attracted thousands of nomads from far and wide. They have set up their tents on the big plain, and all are dressed in their very best clothes. The women are wearing large chunks of amber on their heads and heavy jewelry made from coral, turquoise and agate inherited from their grandmothers and great-grandmothers. The men are wearing coats edged with animal skins and long cutlasses in silver sheaths tucked through their belts. Both villagers and nomads have settled themselves on beautiful woollen rugs spread on the lush meadow grass with its sprinkling of blue and yellow flowers. They have unpacked their brightly coloured leather bags full of *tsampa* (roasted barley flour), bars of *tu* (a mixture of hard cheese, butter and molasses), dried yak meat and crystallized fruits. On a fire made of yak dung, they boil tea in battered kettles. Sitting cross-legged or lying on their sides, men, women and children are all enjoying this brief interlude of summer warmth.

The festival starts. Masked dances, performed by monks, retrace the major events in Gesar's life. Riders in sumptuous costumes, wearing glittering, strangely shaped headdresses, parade about, brandishing victory banners. The story of Gesar is the tale of an invincible warrior whose true enemies were hatred, attachment, arrogance and jealousy. Gesar wielded the sword of knowledge and tore through the veils of ignorance, and his conquests were inner peace and wisdom.

The various episodes relating to Gesar's epic deeds are related in a great many different books (some thirty have been recorded), but the story has spread throughout Tibet and even into Mongolia primarily through the efforts of living storytellers. These modern-day bards are capable of narrating the events of Gesar's life for hours, even days, on end in a continuous singsong, as if they were reading from an inner book. And what is particularly extraordinary is that some of these storytellers are illiterate nomads. This gift for declamation sometimes comes to them quite suddenly, as in the case of one twenty-year-old from Amdo province who starts to sing about the indomitable king's exploits with no prior warning.

When he describes Gesar's miraculous birth, childhood and accession to the throne and other peaceful episodes of his life, his delivery is calm. The miraculous birth of Gesar of Ling from a *nagini*, a half-woman, half-serpent being, is preceded by extraordinary signs: 'A light coating of snow spread a magical carpet over the ground, mottled with red, blue and black, through which golden yellow flowers emerged, and from the sky there fell a rain of white rice whose grains glittered like spangles of silver… Then, from a white vein that opened on the top of the *nagini*'s head, a white egg appeared with three dots that resembled three eyes.'[1] But when he comes to the battles of the conqueror and his followers, and to his descent into hell to deliver the damned, the storyteller's tone rises and his recitation speeds up and becomes more passionate. Gesar, now a grown man and king of Ling, 'seated on a conch throne', cuts a swathe through the demons of suffering:

> *At the eastern tower of hatred's tongues of flame*
> *Oh Wisdom, light your fire,*
> *Soothe the pain of birth.*

> *At the northern tower of anger's dark wind,*
> *Oh Wisdom, light your fire,*
> *Soothe the pain of age.*
> *At the western tower of lechery's waves,*
> *Oh Wisdom, light your fire,*
> *Soothe the pain of sickness.*
> *At the southern tower of pride's immense cavern,*
> *Oh Wisdom, light your fire,*
> *Soothe the pain of death.*[2]

It is an extraordinary experience to hear the storyteller continuing his visionary account for hours on end, with no breaks. Some move from the camps to the villages, particularly during the harsh winter months on the high plateaux, when nomads and peasants have little work to do and so have time to devote to spiritual practice, handicrafts and relaxation. Some wear a special headdress to denote their status and carry a stick decorated with multicoloured silk ribbons and silver pendants. They are offered the hospitality of the village and the whole community gets together to listen to them for a few days. Unfortunately there are fewer and fewer of the more inspired bards who are able to improvise or recite from memory and the majority now rely on the written word to help them.

The Tibetan nomad's real passion in life is horses. Races and equestrian games are therefore a major part of this three-day festival.

The spectators crowd the length of the course or else watch the proceedings from the hillside at the edge of the meadow or perched in little clusters on the roofs of any vehicles parked nearby. A policeman, a monk and a villager teeter together on a narrow bench, precariously balanced, in order to get a better view. When Tibetans organize long-distance races of three or four kilometres, it is painful to watch the way the riders spur on their horses to the point of exhaustion. The fastest animals are real celebrities and their fame spreads throughout the province. Today, during the cavalcade that opens the games, the horses are so frisky on the starting line that even the most experienced riders are having difficulty restraining them. As soon as the signal is given, they are off, hurtling between the packed lines of spectators, whom the officials are struggling to keep off the track. Following this grand opening, the riders take it in turns to ride past again and perform all sorts of acrobatics with their old muskets. Then, spurring their horses into a gallop, they fire blanks at a paper target extended between two posts stuck in the ground. When they hit the bull's eye, a jet of powder shoots out of a cannon and the target collapses in great clouds of white smoke. When they miss, the onlookers laugh good-naturedly.

To bring the morning's proceedings to a close, the riders, still galloping, attempt to scoop up the white silk scarves that have been strewn across the grass of the course. This exercise forces them to lean perilously over to one side in the saddle, to which they are attached only by a length of fabric wound around their thigh. The hardest part, however, is setting themselves upright again with virtually no more than one calf in the saddle.

In the evening, the horses are set loose on the plain. The Khampas have the ability (which I find quite mystifying) to identify their mount almost instantaneously from among the multitude of black, white and brown dots scattered over the meadows and hillsides. Coils of bluish smoke rise up from the tents whose inmates are boiling up fresh noodle soup. Soon the campers fall asleep and the profound silence of the night is broken only, now and then, by dogs warning one another off their own patch or barking at the breeze.

Next day, there is popular dancing from the various regions of Kham. A large number of groups perform, each of them proud of the idiosyncrasies that distinguish their own dances and songs and especially their costumes and jewelry. In the weeks preceding the festival, they have been practising in the fields around their villages or their mountain campsites. Traditional costumes are passed down from one generation to the next: baggy white trousers and red jackets made of wild silk, and variously shaped turbans, for the men; brocades and a whole array of jewelry for the women. Men and women dance first in separate groups, then the groups cross over and reform, each taking it in turn to chant.

But everything has to come to an end. By the evening of the third day, the festival is running out of steam. The tents are folded and the crowd disperses as suddenly as it had appeared, just as the poet Shabkar describes it in the following lines:

When I saw visitors by the thousands
Part from each other and disperse,
It occurred to me that this truly showed
The impermanence of all phenomena.
Like autumn clouds, this life is transient.
Our parents, our relatives, are like passers-by met
    in a marketplace.
Like the dew on grass-tips, wealth is evanescent.
Like a bubble on the surface of water, this body is fragile,
    ephemeral.
The preoccupations of this world are futile;
The spiritual path alone matters.
The chance to engage in it
Occurs only once: right now.

Somewhere deep inside, perhaps they remember that the true festival is the celebration of that unalterable bliss born of meditation and the transformation of the mind.

1 *La Vie surhumaine de Guésar de Ling*, trans. Alexandra David-Neel, Paris: Éditions du Rocher (reprint), 1978, p. 48.
2 *Ibid.*, pp. 115–16.

Horses are the passion of the Tibetan nomads. During the summer festivals, races and equestrian games go on all day long.

Overleaf:
During the Mani Genkok festival, the local beauties wear a huge chunk of amber on their heads and heavy strands of coral, turquoise and agate which have been passed down from one generation to the next.

A policeman, a monk and a villager try to get a better view of the race.

Young Tibetans racing.

The police are present, even though the several thousand nomads have only come to take part in the festival.

Opposite:

A nomad rider firing blanks at a target as he gallops past.

Overleaf:

The Dalai Lama has roundly denounced the recent Tibetan custom of wearing coats edged with panther, tiger and snow leopard fur. He explained that this fashion conflicts with the Buddhist ideals of compassion and non-violence and is contributing to the disappearance of endangered species. Following his injunction, in January 2005, many Tibetans burned their furs in public. 'True ornaments,' the Dalai Lama said, 'are the inner ornaments of altruism, ethics and spiritual practice.'

At the end of the games, the galloping riders bend down to pick up the white scarves strewn across the course.

Opposite:
Caught up in the view through my camera, I stayed a little too long on the racetrack and the leading horse brushed against my shoulder.

Overleaf:
Members of the crowd: a happy little girl, a serene old monk, a respected scholar and a rather flamboyant young boy.

Nomads from the high valleys near Denkok greet our group with smiles. We have helped to build several bridges in the gorges of Tsedrum.

Opposite:
When they are travelling or taking part in festivals, men often have a reliquary hanging from their belt.

Overleaf:
Left: Monks in a tent preparing for the masked dances that tell the story of the great deeds of King Gesar of Ling, the culmination of the Mani Genkok festival.
Right: King Gesar and his men setting off in a grand cavalcade across the plain at Mani Genkok.

Above and opposite:
Pupils of the school which we founded at Shechen performing traditional dances.

Overleaf:
The calm of evening after the day's activities. Several thousand nomads have camped here for the festival.

135

The blocks used to print the texts are cleaned regularly to prevent the ink building up in the grooves.

The Printing Workshop at Derge: A Place Outside Time

It takes three days to engrave the block on both sides.

The Printing Workshop at Derge: A Place Outside Time

'How many hours away is Derge?' The Tibetan driver straightens up and smiles. He is strikingly tall and his long black hair is wound around his head and has pieces of red thread woven into it. A knife in a silver sheath hangs from his belt. He looks at a bit of a loss for an answer. 'Three or four hours', he says, before plunging his arms back into the engine of his four-by-four. On the rather pompously named Sichuan–Tibet Highway, the average speed is around 40 km/h and distances are calculated in an approximate number of hours.

Leaving Mani Gengko, we begin climbing the great Tro-lha pass and our poor old jeep is tested to the limit. The summit is surrounded by glaciers and, rearing in between them, impressive mountains of black rock whose jagged peaks pierce the intense blueness of the sky. The air is thin at this altitude. We breathe in as much as our lungs can take and feel an involuntary wave of euphoria.

Last year, the sign at the top of the pass indicated that we were at 4,950 metres. This year, evidently some progress has been made because the sign, freshly painted, now reads 5,050 metres! So here we are, travelling, by car, 200 metres above the highest mountain in Europe.

After the pass, we begin to descend precipitously through a series of hairpin bends winding beside a seemingly bottomless drop. We pass some pleasant meadowland, then enter the deep gorges that will bring us, in two hours' time, to Derge, a small town anchored between vertiginous cliffs that echo with the roar of a fast-flowing river. Derge, former capital of a small kingdom in the province of Kham, is one of Tibet's major spiritual centres, though it is now attached to the Chinese province of Sichuan and no longer an administrative part of Tibet.

Derge may look somewhat unprepossessing, but it conceals a unique treasure – the largest manual printing workshop in history. It houses hundreds of thousands of engraved wooden tablets on which are printed, not newspapers or novels, but Buddhist texts, historical treatises and works of traditional medicine and astrology. Every aspect of the work, from the engraving to the packing of the books, via the manufacture of ink and paper, is done by hand, employing techniques that have been in use for the last three hundred years. We are going to Derge to buy some rare books on Buddhist philosophy, but not only that: we are also going to immerse ourselves in the atmosphere of a place that feels as if it has escaped time.

In Tibet, books are regarded as 'supports' for the words of the Buddha and of the great scholars and as more precious than images or statues. They must never be placed on the ground or walked or sat upon, but must be kept, as a mark of respect, somewhere high up inside a temple or a house. Merely reading them does not lead to knowledge: they must first be transmitted orally; in other words, we need to hear the text being read aloud by a spiritual master who has himself heard them transmitted in the same way. Then we need to listen to commentaries, also oral, designed to lead the way towards an understanding of the text's meaning. In a country where the word to 'learn' is the same as the word to 'listen', it is sound that transmits knowledge. Reading is a way of using written words to recreate the invisible bridge of meaning which, from mouth to ear and from century to century, connects the reader with the Buddha and with the great interpreters of his words.

The printing workshop was built, for the purpose of printing Buddhist texts, in 1729, by Tenpa Tsering, sixth king of Derge, who was inspired to undertake the project by a series of auspicious dreams. His successor, Phuntsog Tenpa, continued the work of his predecessor by commissioning the engraving of the one hundred and three volumes of the Kangyur, the collected words of the Buddha translated into Tibetan. He then went on to construct a larger building – the one that we see today. Phuntsog Tenpa was concerned that the engraving should be executed with the utmost care, and for some volumes he went so far as to give each workman the quantity of gold dust which could be contained in the cavities of each engraved tablet – the point being that the deeper the engraving, the clearer the resulting letters. Phuntsog Tenpa's efforts were consolidated by later generations, and Derge became the largest printing workshop of its kind in the world. Assuming that a skilled craftsman can engrave one side of a tablet in a day, the 270,000 tablets currently held at Derge – thought to represent three quarters

of Tibet's literary heritage – correspond to the output of ten engravers working over a period of a hundred and fifty years.

On the huge forecourt of the printing workshop, we meet Pewar Rinpoche, one of Derge's most highly respected spiritual masters. Pewar Rinpoche has his long hair knotted on top of his head in a chignon. He is a lay lama and scholar, but also what is known as a *tulku*, the emanation of a past master. With a big smile, he puts round our own heads the traditional white scarf that we have just given him as a sign of pure intention and invites us in.

It is thanks to Pewar Rinpoche and to a doctor called Ngawang Sherap that the printing workshop still exists today. In 1966, at the height of the Cultural Revolution, the Red Guards were on the point of destroying it when the two men shut themselves in the building, barring the heavy doors and nailing up the windows. The brief respite won by this act was to prove crucial. As a result of their action, the Tibetan official in charge of the district, Yarling Dorje, was subjected to a brutal interrogation during which he received four hundred lashes of the whip daily. But in between two torture sessions he succeeded in making telephone contact with a high official in Peking, informing him of the imminent destruction of the printing workshop, together with all the monasteries in the neighbourhood, and asking him to find some means of preventing the disaster.

'Those few days seemed like centuries', recounts Pewar Rinpoche. 'During the night, we managed to pass a number of rare books through the windows so that they could be concealed. We also succeeded in hiding copies of the hundred and three volumes of the Kangyur so that new tablets could be engraved from them if the worst came to the worst. The Communists began by destroying the Derge Gonchen – Derge's major monastery – just next to the printing workshop. But three days later a telegram arrived from Peking. It read: 'Do not destroy the temple or the printing workshop. We must leave an edifying example of the stupidity of the Tibetans, who waste their time in useless spiritual activities.' It was too late for the monastery, but the workshop was saved.

It was not until 1979, however, that the workshop (now protected by the Chinese as a cultural relic) was authorized to open again. In 1987, Tibetans working for the Chinese decided to destroy the ancient building and to erect in its place a concrete edifice to house the books. But Pewar Rinpoche once again saved the printing workshop. He made an impassioned plea in favour of the splendid old building, whose beaten earth walls are two metres thick at the base, arguing that it was part of the cultural heritage not just of Tibet but of the world as a whole. Rather than being destroyed, it should be restored and reinforced. He added that the printing workshop was an object of veneration for the Tibetan people, who came from far and wide to see it – an argument that was unlikely, however, to carry much weight with the Chinese authorities. Pewar Rinpoche also paid a lightning visit to the Panchen Lama, whom the Chinese were still anxious to accommodate at the time. And once again he was successful.

As you step inside the buiilding, the gloom comes as something of a shock after the brightness outside. The workshop has never had electric light because of the potential fire risk, and the traditional windows let in very little natural light. Another thing that strikes the visitor is the atmosphere of feverish activity. A hundred or so workmen are printing sheets of Tibetan paper on long, finely engraved wooden tablets. Around them pages of ancient text are piling up, one by one, on subjects varying from Buddhist philosophy and spiritual practice to biography, medicine, astrology, grammar and poetry. The place is full of the soft sound of rollers creaking as they pass over the paper and monotonous whispering as the workers count off the pages.

The printers work in twos. Sitting opposite one another, they sway rhythmically backwards and forwards, taking it in turns to carry out a series of rapid and precise movements. First they ink the engraved tablet with a brush, then place a sheet of paper on it and press down firmly with a roller. Each pair of printers produces approximately a thousand pages a day. It may seem a lot, but if we remember that the Kangyur is more than 46,000 pages long, we get an idea of the amount of work that the printing of this collection alone entails.

The ink which the printers use is made of mineral pigments. Red is used for the Kangyur and black for the majority of other texts.

The tablets are cleaned regularly in a large wooden trough, and the residues are used to make pills, which are dispensed to pilgrims for their healing properties.

On the upper floors of the building, total silence reigns, and it is here that the engraved tablets are stored and indexed, in a maze of shelves that rise to the ceiling.

In front of the main building, on the other side of the forecourt, is the paper factory. For many years, the Chinese prohibited the use of this handmade paper, forcing the Tibetans to accept industrially produced paper imported from China. Today, however, the paper is again produced by hand, although on a smaller scale than in the past.

The plant from which it is made – *Stellera chamaejasme* – grows in great abundance up in the mountain pastures. The roots of the plant are pounded in a stone trough and the resulting pulp is heated and then stirred in churns similar to those used to prepare butter tea. The mixture is then poured on to a frame of stretched muslin resting on water, and left to dry, after which the finished sheet of paper simply has to be peeled off.

Loaded down with books, we go back to see Pewar Rinpoche and say goodbye. '*Yangmo pe!*' ['Go excellently!'], he says in Khampa dialect as he escorts us to the door, and we reply: '*Kou tsering!*' ['Long life!']. The sound of the jeep's engine starting up seems suddenly incongruous. We have just passed through the invisible barrier. Pewar Rinpoche's smiling face is getting smaller as we pull away, and it seems to say: 'Where are you going in such a hurry?'

The principal statue of the Buddha, known as 'Sangye Gyablongma', at Derge monastery, near the printing workshop. This statue was destroyed during the 'Cultural Revolution', then restored in 1995 thanks to the help of Shechen Rabjam Rinpoche, who had the figure gilded.

Woman wearing traditional Kham jewelry. She has come on a pilgrimage to the printing workshop.

The largest manual printing workshop in history is to be found at Derge, in eastern Tibet. It houses 270,000 engraved wooden blocks containing Buddhist teachings and texts regarding the history of Tibet, medicine and other traditional sciences. The printing workshop was founded in 1729 and miraculously escaped the destruction which reduced 6,000 Tibetan monasteries to dust.

147

Above and opposite:

The printing workshop has been active again for the last twenty-odd years and employs some hundred people. A two-man team can print more than a thousand pages a day. One of them inks the block and lays down a sheet of paper; the other runs the roller over it twice, rapidly, to press the paper on to the engraved block, then lifts off the engraved sheet. Red is used for the Buddhist canon (the 103 volumes of the *Kangyur* containing the teachings of the Buddha) and black for all other texts.

Above and opposite:

The blocks are cleaned every few months. Pills are also made from the red ink, which is prepared from a mineral pigment known for its medicinal properties – enhanced by the salutary effects of the canonical writings themselves.

Dr Lodrö Phuntsok is something of a Renaissance man and has been responsible for reviving traditional arts and Tibetan medicine in the Dzongsar region. He organized the reconstruction of Dzongsar monastery and philosophy school. Here, he is seen holding a bronze statue which has been cast by the lost wax method, a technique that he learnt from Nepalese craftsmen.

The printing workshop is a hive of activity. So many commissions are received from monasteries and from private individuals that months often elapse before an order can be completed.

Above and opposite:

Paper is being produced manually again after a lengthy prohibition by the Chinese government. Tibetan paper is made from the roots of a flowering plant (*Stellera chamaejasme*), which grows very freely in the mountain meadows. The roots are separated into fibres (above), then pounded in a stone trough. The resulting pulp is heated and mixed in churns similar to those used for the preparation of butter tea (left). The mixture is then poured on to muslin stretched over a frame resting on water, and left to dry. The finished sheet of paper is simply peeled off the frame.

A thirteen-year-old apprentice carefully engraving a block of wood. His future is assured thanks to the high demand for books.

A Bhutanese monk copying a text on to a sheet of handmade paper. The art of calligraphy is still very much alive. An experienced calligrapher can write up to fifteen pages a day. His 'pen' is a pointed stick of bamboo and the ink is made from soot taken from the hearth and finely ground, then mixed with water and natural glue.

A monk examines the impression of sacred images printed using large wooden blocks. These images variously represent the succession of a line of sacred masters, different deities of the Buddhist pantheon, mandalas and other aids to meditation.

There are several floors of corridors like this, housing hundreds of thousands of wooden printing blocks. This monk, on pilgrimage from Nepal, has placed a block on his head as a sign of respect and in order to receive its blessing.

Opposite:

Pewar Rinpoche, who saved the printing workshop on two occasions. The first was during the Cultural Revolution, when he barricaded himself inside the building with another monk, and the second, in 1985, when the authorities wanted to replace it with a modern building in concrete.

Right:

A calligrapher copies the text for engraving on to tracing paper. The transparent paper will then be glued on to the wood block and the engravers will hollow out the wood between the inked letters, thereby throwing them into relief.

Overleaf:

The icy lake of Yilung Lhatso (4,300 m), not far from Derge. It was given the name, meaning 'Divine Lake of the Mind's Delight', in memory of a Tibetan princess who came to be married in the Derge region and was so entranced by the beauty of the place that she decided to stay. The engraving on the rock reads 'Om Mani Padme Hum', which is the mantra of the Buddha of Compassion.

A monk looks out over the high valley of the Yangtse, at the level of Dengkok. The Yangtse rises on the high plateaux of eastern Tibet, where it is known as the Drichu. Two celebrated masters of Tibetan Buddhism were born here: to the left (south) of the valley, Dilgo Khyentse Rinpoche (1910–91), and to the right (north), the 16th Karmapa (1924–82).

A Visit to the Mountain Hermit

This hermit from Denkok valley has spent twelve years living as a total recluse. He has followed the custom of leaving his hair to grow rather than wasting time in trivial activities like hair-cutting.

A Visit to the Mountain Hermit

We have been climbing the same steep path edged with juniper bushes for three hours now. Earlier, we were walking through meadows full of gentians and furry white edelweiss that seemed to be inviting us to stay and relax. The Drichu river, which rises on the high Tibetan plateaux and flows into China as the Yangtse, already seems very far away, down there in the great valley that it crosses and waters. The air is bracing, and at 4,500 metres the brilliant blue of the sky bounces sharply off the bright rocks, more intense up here than it ever is on the plains. We are approaching the caves where some dozen hermits, monks, nuns and lay practitioners lead a quiet life of contemplation in a silence only broken intermittently, as if to emphasize its profoundness, by the cry of a marmot, the raucous shriek of a raven or the fluting of a thrush. This place is called 'the Lotus Meadow'. In the words of Kalden Gyatso, a hermit greatly revered in Amdo:

> If you aspire to mountain solitudes
> Under peaks wrapped in mist,
> There are natural caves in steep, rocky cliffs.
> To stay in such places will bring immediate and ultimate joy.

The local nomads sometimes come to visit the hermits and enjoy the opportunity to share in their life by providing for their meagre needs, bringing them *tsampa* (roasted barley flour), butter and dried meat, which they will leave at the entrance to the hermitage if the practitioner is on a closed retreat.

We approach one of the caves, which opens on to a little sunny ledge. Our two guides, a monk from the monastery in the valley and a practitioner of traditional Tibetan medicine, know the hermits well and know that the particular hermit who lives here is prepared to receive the odd pilgrim who may be passing this way. The cave has been very simply arranged, divided up by the addition of a few low stone walls to create separate living spaces. Stooping to pass through the entrance, we find ourselves in a tiny antechamber where the only objects to be seen are a clay hearth, a pile of dry wood, an aluminium kettle and a few canvas bags containing provisions.

Two steps take us up to a heavy linen curtain, and in the room behind we encounter the hermit. It is just possible to stand upright in the middle of the room, which is feebly lit by a skylight. On one side, a small altar has been improvised in the black rock. On the other is a simple stone wall plastered with earth and, at floor level, a bed where the hermit sleeps at night and sits in the day. At the head of the bed, on a rustic shelf, is a pile of books wrapped in material of various colours: books of spiritual instruction, biographies of great teachers and a few philosophical works. Each of them is made up of a series of oblong unbound sheets that have either been handwritten or printed from engraved wood blocks like those used at the Derge workshop.

The hermit greets us calmly but warmly. He is thirty-six and has been on retreat in this cave for four years. After studying for several years in a monastery in the valley, where he acquired the title of *khenpo* (the equivalent of doctor of philosophy), he felt a deep desire to devote himself to meditation. He was anxious to escape the worldly preoccupations that oppress so many of us – the concern with acquiring and losing things, with praise and blame, and status and the lack of it, with feelings of pleasure and disappointment.

He gives us tea, or, to be more precise, hot water with a few tea leaves floating on top. In the quietly contemplative atmosphere of the cave, weighty conversations seem out of place. We ask simply about his health, exchange a few words about spiritual practice, and promise to send him a book that he wants which we have had reprinted in India. Then, after sharing his silence for a while, we take our leave, and as we go we put down a little money, discreetly, to help him pursue his ascetic life.

Not far away, sheltered by an overhang, there is a small ledge that looks out over a sweeping panorama. A mat has been spread across some pine branches, and it appears that the hermit comes to sit here sometimes, letting his mind mingle with the sky and embrace the immensity of nature spread before him.

We now go on down to the main cave – the cave that has made the 'Lotus Meadow' a place of pilgrimage. It was here that Guru Padmasambhava is said to have meditated when he came to Tibet to pass on the Buddha's teachings, at the end of the 8th and beginning of the 9th century. More than a thousand years later, another spiritual master and a rather unconventional figure, Patrul Rinpoche (1806–87), also made a retreat here. It was in this same cave that he wrote a poem, famous throughout Tibet, teaching the impermanence of all life. The poem tells the story of a young bee that has become imprisoned inside the flower where she was gathering honey, and the despair of her fiancé, who tries in vain to free her.

Patrul Rinpoche was one of the most highly revered spiritual teachers of eastern Tibet. His memory is still very much alive and the celebrated *Words of My Perfect Teacher*, one of his many writings, is a constant source of inspiration for practitioners of Tibetan Buddhism. He owned absolutely nothing and wandered through the mountains, living in caves, forests and remote hermitages. He would stop in a place simply to meditate, then move on with no particular destination in mind. He focused constantly on the qualities of compassion and love of others and would repeat to everyone he met: 'Have a good heart and act with kindness: there is nothing more important than that.'

Patrul Rinpoche was also a great scholar, known as a man of few words who went directly to the heart of the Buddhist teachings. He made no concessions to the affairs of the world and was not particularly approachable. And yet those who lived with him for any length of time found it extraordinarily difficult to leave him.

Nothing in his appearance distinguished him from an ordinary nomad. In fact, on one occasion, a lama who failed to recognize him gave him instruction regarding his own writings! Patrul Rinpoche never accepted gifts and if anyone insisted on giving him something valuable – gold, silver, or jewels – he just left it where it was and went quietly on his way.

It is now time for us to retrace our steps. How much easier it is going down than going up, especially at this altitude! An hour and a half later, we are back in the village. We are exhausted and our legs are trembling, but we feel a sense of quiet satisfaction as a result of our pilgrimage. But a few flowers picked at the entrance to the cave and dried in a notebook will allow us to return there later in our thoughts.

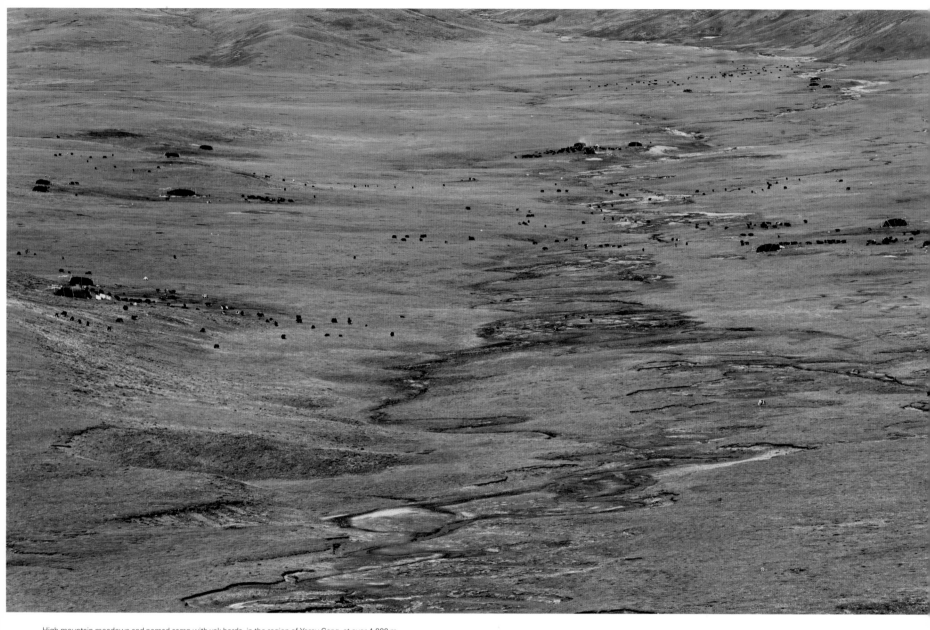

High mountain meadows and nomad camp with yak herds, in the region of Yerey Gang, at over 4,000 m.

Opposite:
A reincarnated lama rides to a mountain monastery above the Sakar valley.

Overleaf:
Left: Khyentse Rinpoche greeting one of his old friends, on his first return to Tibet, in 1985, after over thirty years in exile. This friend was retreat master at the famous Kangri Thokar hermitages, in central Tibet. Both men spent a great many years living in seclusion.
Right: A great yogi and hermit, Tokden Amten, who largely devoted himself to a life of solitary contemplation.

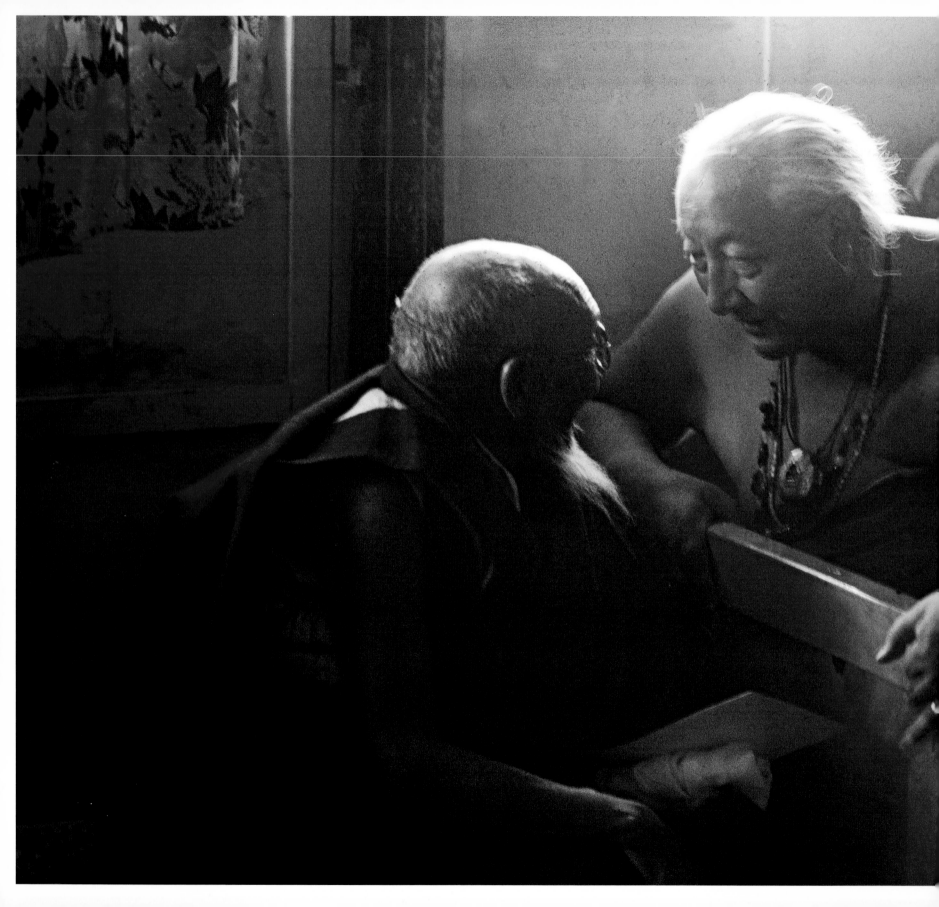

Left:

A ninety-three-year-old Tibetan hermit. He was the retreat master at the Tsadra Rinchen Dra hermitages, above Palpung monastery, in eastern Tibet.

Opposite:

A monk from Shechen monastery at the end of the traditional retreat that lasts three years, three months and three days.

Overleaf:

The Annapurna massif seen from the retreat centre of Pema Osel Ling, the 'land of the lotus of light', at Namo Buddha in Nepal.

Dilgo Khyentse Rinpoche (1910–91) was a model spiritual master, a fountain of love and wisdom for all those who came into contact with him, and a man who had achieved a rare level of understanding through the pursuit of his own inner journey. He was extraordinarily erudite, but in addition to scholarly learning he had the advantage of some thirty years spent in solitary contemplation. During the latter part of his life, he taught constantly, sharing his knowledge with countless disciples, and was one of the principal masters of the Dalai Lama.

Mount Bahla, which dominates the Denkok valley. On the left side of the escarpment is a cave where Khyentse Rinpoche spent an entire winter, at 4,700 metres, cut off from the rest of the world by snow.

Mount Bahla in moonlight.

The Drichu valley. (The river becomes the Yangtse in China.) A great many contemplatives and spiritual masters have lived in caves and hermitages on the sides of these hills.

The cave of the great Indian sage Padampa Sangye, in the Sakar valley, to which Khyentse Rinpoche retired for a year in the 1930s.

Opposite:
An almost lunar landscape near Tawu, in Kham.

Overleaf:
These hermits have all spent many years living in seclusion.

Previous pages:

Left: A monk meditating in the Pema Rithang cave, in the high Drichu valley. Patrul Rinpoche (1808–87),
a famous spiritual teacher, lived and meditated here.
Right: A monk meditating at the entrance to the Citadel of the Tigress (Takmo Dzong),
in Golok province, in north-east Tibet. This cave was inhabited for several years by the famous
Tibetan yogi Shabkar (1781–1851).

Above:

The cliff of Jadrön, in Amdo province. In the 18th century, the yogi Shabkar spent a year's retreat
in a cave in the cliff face at the age of eighteen.

Right:

A visit to the cave in the Bahla cliff, at 4,700 m, where Dilgo Khyentse Rinpoche meditated during his youth.

Overleaf:

The serene landscape of the high plateaux near Sinda monastery.

This rocky peak, strewn with prayer flags, overlooks the Machen region, at Dzogyen Rawa, in Golok province.

On the Roof of the World

The idyllic Dophu valley, near Dzongsar, on the pilgrimage route
to the 'Lake of Turquoise where the Snow Lioness Roars'.

On the Roof
of the World

'I raised my head, looking up,
And saw the cloudless sky.
I thought of absolute space, free from limits,
I then experienced a freedom
Without centre, without end.'
Shabkar

It is July, the rainy season. Three days ago, we left the interminable grey suburbs of Chengdu and the muggy heat of the Chinese plains. We travelled to Datsedo (Kangding to the Chinese), former frontier town between China and eastern Tibet, which lies at 2,800 metres. It was via Datsedo that the Tibetans used to get the blocks of black tea which they use in the preparation of their favourite drink – a salty concoction known as butter tea.

As we climb higher, the sky becomes clearer, more blue, and the air is dry and bracing. Even our minds seem to clear, becoming calm and free from the usual hankerings, eager only to gaze at this astonishing landscape that spreads before our eyes. At the Jara Lhatse pass, at over 4,000 metres, we leave the conifer forests behind and enter a completely different world, one of huge grassy plateaux where yaks and sheep and goats with amazing horns graze, and where nomad tents suddenly appear out of nowhere, and riders come galloping over carpets of flowers. The landscape that meets our eyes seems to go on for ever, extraordinarily beautiful, the purity of the air giving it a sharpness of focus that looks unreal.

Travellers must alter their points of reference and adjust to the sheer scale of it all. To the south, Minyak Kangkar (7,556 metres) rarely emerges from its palace of clouds. To the west, the road rises rapidly towards the immense Tibetan plateau, where the line of eternal snows begins higher than the summit of Mont Blanc. From June to August, the east Tibetan province of Kham is an undulating expanse of pasture lands carpeted with flowers. Buttercups come first, followed by gentians, sweet marjoram and edelweiss, and for these few months Kham is paradise.

Coils of smoke are rising from some twenty tents made of thick black material woven from yak hair. The children have just returned with the animals after letting them graze all day on the grassy slopes. Now it is time for milking. The dri (female yaks) and the dzomo (females born of a yak and a cow) are tied together in a line. All the women then set about collecting the two or three litres of milk that each animal gives each evening. The milk will be used mainly for making butter and dried cheese. When almost all the milk has been taken from one animal, her calf (which is tied up during the milking process) is set loose and allowed to drain the last few mouthfuls left in its mother's udder. It needs no encouragement and suckles greedily.

When we approach one of the tents, the mother of the household, sister to one of the monks at Shechen, invites us in with a big smile. Occupying the middle of the tent is a fireplace, with an opening in the tent above (only closed when it pours with rain) for the smoke to escape through. Thick, hard, flat cushions covered in woollen rugs are scattered all around it. At the back, there is a pile of bales. A butter lamp is burning on an altar, throwing its golden light over a statue of the Buddha and photographs of the Dalai Lama and the spiritual masters of the region.

Nomads generally move camp four times a year, at the start of each season. At the beginning of summer, they take their herds up to an altitude of 4,500 metres. When autumn approaches, they come back down again to look for whatever decent expanse of green grass they can still find. In the winter, some nomads stay in their tents; others move to houses built of mud and during the day take their herds to places where the wind blows off the covering snow, revealing a few tufts of grass burnt by the frost. They invite one or two monks to read the holy books to them for a week or two, and they themselves spend more time, on these long cold days, reciting prayers and mantras and doing great numbers of prostrations.

The winters are exceptionally harsh. The temperature often drops to –30°C, sometimes even –40°C. Lakes and rivers are covered with a thick layer of ice over which humans, animals and vehicles can travel without risk. Both men and women wear thick coats made of a number of sheepskins sewn together. Cheeks are reddened and burnt by the wind and lips are cracked. Inside the home, families gather around a brazier to warm fingers that are stiffened with the cold. In the morning, when seven bowls of fresh water are placed as an offering before the statue of the Buddha on the family altar, barely

has the last bowl been filled than the first is already frozen over. Fortunately, the sky is often brilliantly clear at this time of year and the days are sunny, and this dry cold is more bearable than the penetrating dampness of the Himalayan foothills.

In western Tibet, in the region of Mount Kailash, the landscape is quite different. Huge arid plateaux seem to go on for ever, bordered in the south by the lofty snows of the Himalayas and separated by passes that continue one behind the other to the edge of sight. Not much grows here beyond a scattering of gaunt bushes and the wild grasses that ripple in the wind. In the vicinity of a river, the landscape is softened by patches of green, but most of the region's inhabitants have never even seen a tree. Very occasionally, travellers may stumble upon a little clump of willow trees in a moist, sheltered valley. In some places, the minerals in the rocks can produce extraordinary colours, contrasting dramatically with the turquoise lakes set in the landscape like shining jewels. Dazzlingly white clouds blow up and disperse again in the blue depths of the sky. A few villages built of mud are all that the traveller is likely to encounter, and from time to time scattered nomads who live even more simply that those of Kham.

The landscape of western Tibet has a kind of grandiose monotony, in the midst of which vistas of extraordinary splendour suddenly open up – like that of Mount Kailash, seen from the top of a pass, with the vast blue expanse of Lake Manasarovar at its feet. Kailash, the 'Silver Mountain', known to the Tibetans as 'the White Mountain of the

Snows', or Kangkar Tise, is one of the holiest places in the East, revered by Hindus and Buddhists alike. Pilgrimages to Mount Kailash have been going on for centuries. As Lama Govinda writes in The Way of the White Clouds, 'some mountains are just mountains, but others have a personality and thereby the power to influence men. The greatest of all, since the beginning of time, was and remains Mount Kailash.'

The circumambulation of the sacred mountain begins in the little village of Darchen. The Tibetan pilgrims leave at around three o'clock in the morning and complete the sixty-five-kilometre circuit by nightfall. To do this, they have to traverse a pass of 5,860 metres, an altitude at which breathing becomes difficult and every step is an effort. Those who do the journey by prostrating themselves along the route take about three weeks to complete the circuit. Foreign visitors usually take three days. The route is scattered with caves and hermitages where, over the years, a great many people have come to live simply and to meditate.

Some pilgrims also undertake the three- to four-day circuit of Lake Manasarovar, visiting the caves and monasteries along its shores. Situated at 4,600 metres, Manasarovar – also known as 'the Invincible Turquoise Lake', 'the Lake of Eternal Freshness' and 'the Lake of the Divine Lotus' – is the highest freshwater lake in the world and a place of indescribable beauty. To the south are the majestic snow peaks of the Gurla Mandata, rising to 7,600 metres. To the north is the summit of Mount Kailash, whose solitary grandeur allows the human mind a glimpse of infinite peace.

The lake is bordered by marshes covered in brightly coloured plants – orange, dark green and brick red – and beaches of black sand. To sit beside it is to let one's mind merge effortlessly with space and silence, its perfection underlined by the haunting cry of a wild duck. The sound seems so close but comes from half a kilometre away. The great Tibetan yogi Shabkar (1781–1851) writes: 'One day when I was resting at the lakeside, I experienced a freedom liberated from all thought, a clear, vast and open state. The experience inspired the following song:

The mind given back to itself,
Ample as space, transparent and serene,
The painful attachments of mental labour
Loosen themselves of their own accord.

When I dwell in this state,
Empty, limpid sky,
I know a joy that goes beyond word,
Thought and expression.

Compassion towards all beings,
My mothers of long ago, streamed up from deep inside me;
These are not empty words:
From now on, I shall devote myself to the good of others!

Through its people, its culture and its landscapes, the Roof of the World remains a source of inspiration and hope for humanity. It has, it is true, reached an unstable frontier point between tradition and modernity. If it is capable of maintaining the essence of its traditions and its Buddhist culture, while also adopting the positive benefits of the modern world in terms of health and improvement in living conditions, then it will have successfully negotiated the transition and will continue to make a contribution to the fund of human knowledge and resources. To do this, it will have to face the double challenge of resisting excessive Chinese influence and also those cultural trends that are driving it in the direction of Western commercialism at its worst. Over the centuries, Buddhists, and in particular practitioners of Tibetan Buddhism, have developed an art of meditation and living whose value and effectiveness are now beginning to be studied and recognized by top specialists in the field of neuroscience. Its emphasis on the training and transformation of the mind has conferred a very special quality on Tibetan civilization. As the Dalai Lama frequently reminds us, this heritage is not exclusive to six million Tibetans: it is the heritage of humanity as a whole. As such, it deserves to be safeguarded. What is more, having been conquered from without by a foreign power, the Tibetans must guard against being dominated from within by the more negative aspects of the contemporary world: the insatiable quest for money, power, status and material conditions which, alone, cannot ensure permanent wellbeing. The future alone will tell whether the compassionate gaze of Tibet's spiritual masters is still able to illuminate the world and whether the Tibetans themselves are still able to appreciate its true worth.

The sacred valley of Dakpa Lhari, the 'pure, divine mountain', south of Lithang, in Kham province.

Previous pages:

Left: A small lake set like a turquoise in the landscape of western Tibet, not far from Mount Kailash.

Right: In parts of western Tibet, the rocks are brightly coloured due to the presence of various minerals.

Above:

The Makalu (7,668 m) seen from the air during a flight from Kathmandu to Lhasa.

At an altitude of 4,600 m, Lake Manasarovar (surface area 320 km²) is the highest freshwater lake in the world. Situated near Mount Kailash and the Gurla Mandata, which rises to over 7,000 m (and can be seen in the photograph), it is also known as the 'Lake of Eternal Freshness'. Pilgrims take four days to walk around the sacred lake.

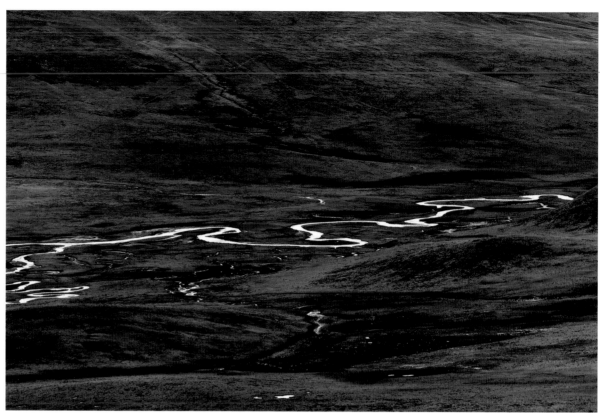

High mountain meadows in the Jomda region.

Opposite:
Aerial view of terraced fields in Amdo province (Qinhai).

Pages 206–7
A rock covered with mantras: a frequent sight in the Himalayas.

Pages 208–9
The Zitsa Degu valley, better known to the Chinese and to foreign visitors by its Chinese name, Jiuzhaigou, lies in eastern Tibet, on the former frontier between Tibet and China (now part of Sichuan province). It offers an extraordinary panorama of colourful lakes and spectacular waterfalls that cover an area of some fifty kilometres.

Previous pages:
Monks from the monastery-hermitage of Yama Tashikhyil, in Amdo, at dusk.

Above:
The master arrives as night falls and is received by a procession of monks, who escort him to his residence.

Opposite:
A great master, Kyabje Trulshik Rinpoche, has come to pay these monks a visit and is greeted with clouds of sweet smoke from branches of burning juniper.

Overleaf:
Left: The monastery of Thangboche in Khumbu province, Nepal, at sunset.
Right: Mount Kailash, the 'Silver Mountain', known to the Tibetans as the 'White Mountain of the Snows', or Kangkar Tise, is revered by Hindus and Buddhists alike and regarded as one of the holiest mountains. It has been home to a great many hermits, including the great Milarepa (1040–1123).

Nomads, dressed in thick sheepskins (although it is summer), wait beside the road amid clouds of incense smoke. They have come to greet Dilgo Khyentse Rinpoche on his return to eastern Tibet (Kham) after more than thirty years' exile.

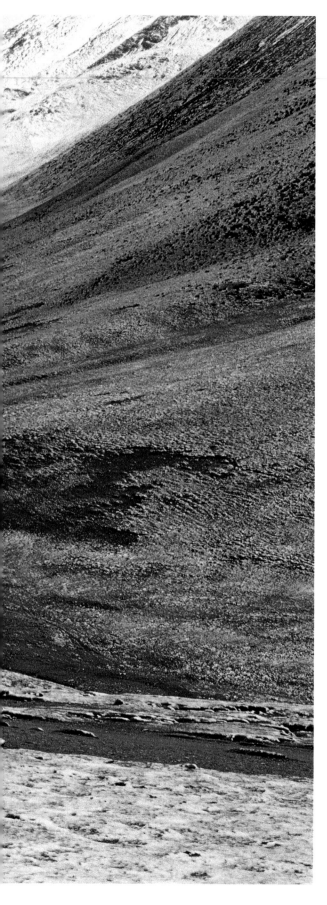

Valley near Dzogchen in eastern Tibet.

Opposite:
Countryside around the holy mountain of Machen. It is early August and snow is falling.

Overleaf:
Left: The sacred lake of Manasarovar, at 4,600 m.
Right: Horses under a cloudy sky, at 4,800 m, near Bayang in western Tibet. They are heading for Mount Kailash.

219

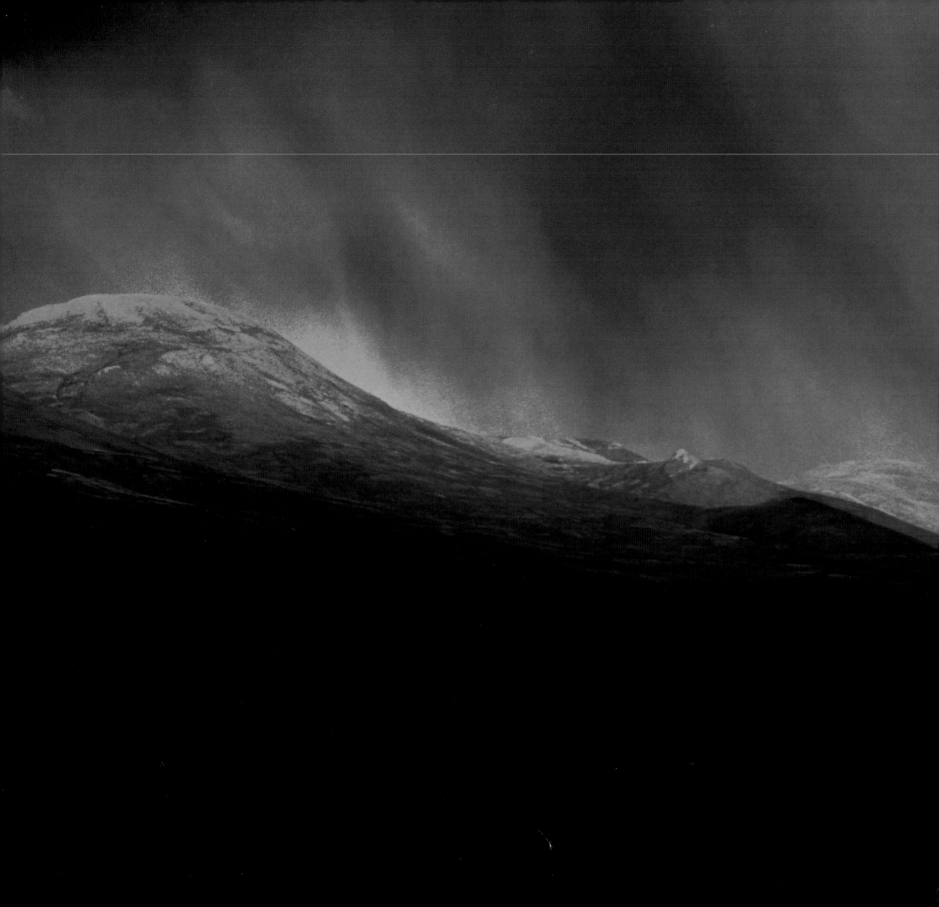

Previous pages:
The earth and the sky seem to meet at Bayang, in western Tibet.

Opposite:
A stormy sky in the Yerey Gang region, between Jomda and Sinda, in eastern Tibet.

Below:
Monk making an offering of juniper incense.

Overleaf:
In eastern Tibet, at 4,000 m, the meadows are carpeted with flowers, yellow in July and blue in August.
A pyramid of prayer flags can be seen here in the middle distance. Dzachuka region.

Some of the 160 pupils attending the school we built for nomad children in the Shechen valley, in eastern Tibet.

In the Service of the Land of the Snows

We travelled all day at an altitude of 4,000 metres without seeing a single road. This is a remote region of eastern Tibet which I visit every year as part of a programme of humanitarian projects that we have developed in the Land of the Snows. We crossed meadows carpeted with colourful wild flowers and littered with holes and small mounds that are the work of tens of thousands of abras (similar to the pikas of North America). These tail-less rodents are appealing little creatures, but the underground galleries they excavate create havoc in all the grazing lands that they colonize.

We climbed lush hillsides to avoid getting bogged down in the marshes. And we crossed overflowing rivers with our hearts in our mouths. The Tibetans have a special talent for these river crossings. After checking for tyre marks left by other vehicles, they gauge the level of the water (a few days of rain are enough to raise it to the point where a crossing is impossible), then they enter the current, at just the right speed, neither not too fast, nor too slow. At the point when the water almost reaches the windows and begins pouring into the car, most of the passengers hold their breath. Others start reciting mantras. The daredevils just laugh.

Last summer, during one of these many crossings, the current was so strong that we felt the car being lifted and swept along several metres. There were a few moments of intense expectation, when the water came over the top of the bonnet, followed by sighs of relief and whoops of joy as we reached the opposite bank. A lone wolf, on a nearby hill, had observed the whole incident.

At dusk, at last, we reached our destination, the little monastery of Sida, near which we have built a school. The next morning we visited the nomad communities who live locally. We went into one tent, made of woven yak hair, where a young girl was cooking little pieces of cheese in a cauldron over a clay hearth in the centre. She was stirring the contents of the pot with a big wooden spoon. The sun's rays were playing with the blue smoke that escaped slowly through an opening in the roof. The young girl's grandmother was sitting in a corner saying prayers, and to one side of the tent Lhamo, the girl's mother, was lying on a small mattress. She looked incredibly frail. Her eyes were too big for her thin face and they had a strangely fixed look.

When Lhamo fell ill, she was taken on horseback to a small hospital two days' journey from here. She was diagnosed as suffering from tuberculosis of the bones, but her family could not afford to buy the medicines needed to cure her. Lhamo's condition deteriorated and for the past three months she had been bedridden. Her husband had died the previous year, and her elderly mother and thirteen-year-old daughter now had to manage everything on their own.

Fortunately, we had brought enough medicine in our bags for Lhamo to receive treatment for the next year. We explained carefully to her daughter how to administer the drugs. She listened attentively, her face betraying a mixture of disbelief and the faintest glimmer of hope. The grandmother thanked us profusely amidst mumbled prayers, struggling to hold back her tears.

We have met a great many patients in eastern Tibet suffering from serious illnesses, with little hope of a cure. And yet there are things we can do for these sick people. Despite the difficult conditions, since 2000 we have succeeded in building sixteen small clinics, ten schools, nine bridges and two retirement homes for the elderly. Each clinic has five or six rooms, a doctor living on site with his family, an assistant carer and a stock of medicines. These dispensaries are pretty basic by modern-day standards, generally having no electricity or running water, but they are still better than nothing.

Tibetan doctors who have received a rudimentary medical training in the hospitals founded by the Chinese government have a tendency to over-treat patients and to resort too freely to intravenous injections. But a process has begun and lives are being saved. Our growing network of medical centres provides a base for further developments. The bridges we have built have improved the lives of local people considerably. In 2005, for example, we built a bridge over the Yangtse (which the Tibetans call the Drichu) in a region where no safe means of crossing existed for almost a hundred kilometres. People living nearby used to use flimsy little boats, which were not adequate to cope with the current, and each year the river claimed a number of lives.

In 2005, we went back to Lhamo's yak-hair tent. We already knew that she had survived her illness, but otherwise we did not know quite what to expect. We might quite easily have mistaken this radiantly smiling woman for someone else. Lhamo had put on weight and was now walking with two wooden sticks, next to her daughter, whose affection could not have been more apparent. To save a life, even just one life, makes all our efforts worthwhile.

Above:
Lying in her tent, looking a little like a discarded doll, Lhamo receives her first treatment for tuberculosis.

Below:
Lhamo a year later, with her daughter.

Young orphan girl at the school at Dzogyen Rawa, in Golok.

Acknowledgments

My sincere thanks to all of those who have contributed to the creation of this book:

Rabjam Rinpoche, the abbot of Shechen monastery and the spiritual heir of Dilgo Khyentse Rinpoche, whom I had the good fortune to accompany on his journeys to Tibet.

My publisher, Hervé de La Martinière, who was warm and enthusiastic throughout the making of this book, as well as Emmanuelle Halkin, the editor, Audrey Hette, the designer, and all our other friends at Editions de La Martinière.

The Donald and Shelley Rubin Foundation and the Tsadra Foundation, who generously provided me with the best photographic equipment possible.

Raphaële Demandre, who works with me and all our Tibetan friends on the humanitarian projects that we run on the Roof of the World. She often photographed the same scenes as I did and could easily have been the author of this book.

Carisse Busquet who carefully read through the text, as well as Christian Bruyat for his contribution to the chapter on the Derge printing workshop.

Chimé Leschly and the late Tenzin Gyaltsen who worked with us on the Shechen Archives, at our monastery in Nepal.

Yann Arthus-Bertrand, who generously gave us his help and advice on many occasions.

Pierre Botte and Dave Long who kindly scanned some of our silver-plate images, and Vivian Kurz who tirelessly assists us with all our publishing projects.

The author's share of the proceeds from this book has been entirely donated to various humanitarian projects in Tibet, Nepal, India and Bhutan, under the inspiration of Shechen Rabjam Rinpoche. To find out more about this work, please contact:

Dilgo Khyentse Fellowship
109 Mowbray Drive
Kew Gardens, NY 11415
USA
shechen@sprynet.com
www.shechen.org

The photographs in this book are also available as signed limited-edition prints. For more details, please go to www.shechen.org

Translated from the French *Tibet, regards de compassion* by Ruth Sharman

First published in the United Kingdom in 2006 by Thames & Hudson Ltd, 181A High Holborn, London WC1V 7QX

www.thamesandhudson.com

First published in 2006 in hardcover in the United States of America by Thames & Hudson Inc., 500 Fifth Avenue, New York, New York 10110

thamesandhudsonusa.com

Original version © 2006 Éditions de La Martinière, Paris
This edition © 2006 Thames & Hudson Ltd, London

British Library Cataloguing-in-Publication Data
A catalogue record for this book is available from the British Library

Library of Congress Catalog Card Number 2006905210

ISBN-13: 978-0-500-54332-0
ISBN-10: 0-500-54332-1

Printed and bound in France by Pollina - L40604B